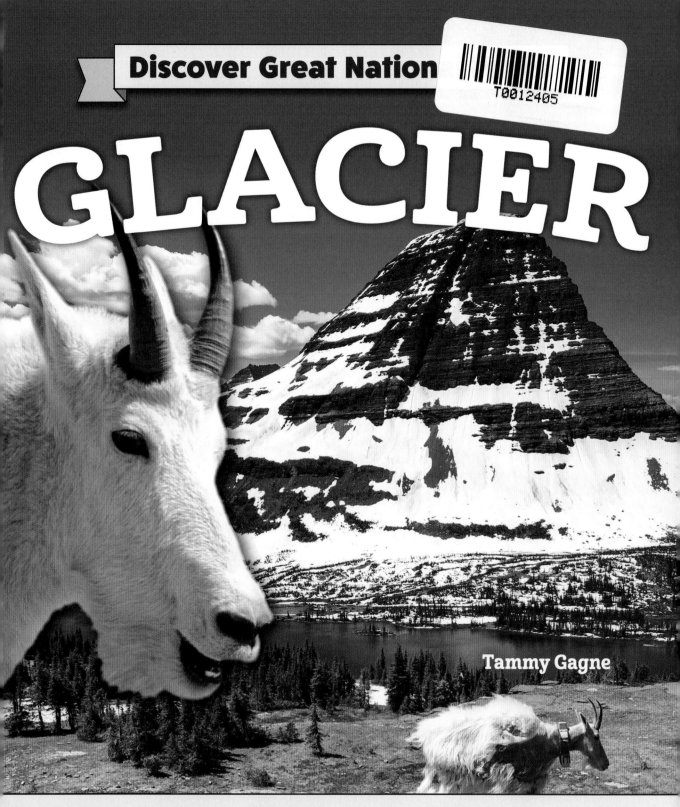

T0012405

Discover Great Nation

GLACIER

Tammy Gagne

Kids' Guide to History, Wildlife, Trails, and Park Preservation

© 2024 by Curious Fox Books™, an imprint of Fox Chapel Publishing Company, Inc., 903 Square Street, Mount Joy, PA 17552.

Discover Great National Parks: Glacier is a revision of *Glacier*, published in 2017 by Purple Toad Publishing, Inc. Reproduction of its contents is strictly prohibited without written permission from the rights holder.

Paperback ISBN 979-8-89094-064-3
Hardcover ISBN 979-8-89094-065-0

The Cataloging-in-Publication Data in on file with the Library of Congress.

To learn more about the other great books from Fox Chapel Publishing, or to find a retailer near you, call toll-free 800-457-9112 or visit us at www.FoxChapelPublishing.com.

We are always looking for talented authors. To submit an idea, please send a brief inquiry to acquisitions@foxchapelpublishing.com.

Fox Chapel Publishing makes every effort to use environmentally friendly paper for printing.

Printed in China

WELCOME

CHAPTER ONE
THE CROWN OF THE CONTINENT

Each year, millions of people travel to the northwest corner of Montana to visit Glacier National Park, where knife-edged mountain peaks reach into the sky, giving the park its nickname, "The Crown of the Continent." These remarkable rock faces rise from lush green valleys, carved into the northern Rocky Mountains over millennia by the slow-moving advance and retreat of sheets of glacial ice. To visit Glacier is to see what it is like to travel back in time through layers of exposed geology and acres of deep wilderness. The views in all directions are incredible, from turquoise lakes and dense forests to the rugged rock faces punctuated by waterfalls and the few remaining glaciers.

Among the most popular vacation spots in the United States, Glacier is among the top ten most visited national parks. Covering more than a million acres of land, it stretches north to Canada where it conjoins its sister park, Waterton Lakes, to form the Glacier-Waterton International Peace Park. Wild rivers, miles of hiking trails, boating, and red-jammer bus tours await the adventurer.

St. Mary Lake is the typical teal color of a glacier lake.

5

Glacier National Park is big in almost every way. It includes 762 lakes and 175 mountains. Its largest lake, Lake McDonald, covers 6,823 acres. The tallest mountain, Mount Cleveland, measures 10,448 feet tall.[1] The only thing small about the park is the number of glaciers—at least compared to the number that used to be found there. Of the 150 glaciers found in the park in 1850, only twenty-five remain today.[2]

Going-to-the-Sun Road winds east to west through the heart of the park. Visitors who drive it can see breathtaking views without

Mount Cleveland is the highest mountain in Glacier National Park. It is part of the Lewis Range, which stretches northward into Canada.

In the summer months, the sharp ridge known as the Garden Wall is flanked by many different types of wildflowers.

ever leaving their cars. In the early evening, the sun makes the road glow gold. Going east, the road climbs higher up into the mountains. Huge rock formations, such as the Garden Wall, can be seen from the road. Dazzling waterfalls, like Bird Woman Falls, cascade over the massive rocks.

The highest spot that an automobile can reach is Logan Pass. This is where Going-to-the-Sun Road crosses the Continental Divide. This natural boundary line runs all the way from Alaska to South America. It separates the waters that flow into the Atlantic Ocean from those heading to the Pacific Ocean. In the United States, the Continental Divide follows the crest of the Rocky Mountains.

Winter activities, like snowshoeing and cross-country skiing, are very popular in Glacier National Park.

Winters are fierce in Glacier National Park. Snow and ice shuts down long stretches of roads from late September until late June. Then, in July and August, the land comes back to life. Colorful wildflowers seem to pop up overnight, dotting the valleys. Cottonwoods and aspen trees leaf out once again. Even the many conifers—trees that keep their needles all year long—seem a little greener at this time of year. Led by their parents, baby animals born in the spring start exploring.

Many types of animals live in Glacier National Park year-round, and more than sixty different mammal species call the park home. Luckily for the tourists, the grizzly bears keep mostly to themselves, and the gray wolves stay away too. But many campers and hikers often encounter other kinds of animals. They may see bighorn sheep, deer, elk, moose, and mountain goats.

Tourists interested in bird watching should keep an eye out for bald eagles. The national bird can be spotted flying overhead or diving into the lakes in search of fish. The eagle is just one of more than 260 bird species that live in Glacier National Park.

The many different types of animals and plants in the park make it one of the largest and most beautiful ecosystems in the world. It is one of the many reasons the land was named a national park.

A grizzly strolls through Glacier.

A bull moose stands in a meadow.

A bald eagle.

Chapter Two
Creating a
National Park

Glacier National Park became the country's tenth national park on May 11, 1910. It was largely thanks to a man named George Bird Grinnell. Grinnell discovered his love of nature as a young boy. He and his family moved to Audubon Park in New York, which was a fourteen-acre area of Manhattan that was still wooded. Grinnell's life changed when he met Lucy Bakewell Audubon, a widow of the well-known ornithologist, naturalist, and painter, John James Audubon. Mrs. Audubon shared her husband's love for birds. She taught what she knew about various birds to many children at a small school. Grinnell was one of her young students.

As an adult, Grinnell earned two degrees from Yale University. He became one of the country's most outspoken activists about the wonder of nature. He also founded the Audubon Society, a group dedicated to protecting nature. He named it after his teacher's late husband.

In 1875, Grinnell traveled to the newly opened Yellowstone Park. Along the way, he noted forty mammals

In Glacier National Park, hidden lakes are treasures discovered by hikers and campers.

11

and 139 bird species. He saw that some animals were in serious trouble due to poaching. If people did nothing to help them, he feared some of the species would be lost forever.

Grinnell realized that too much hunting was being allowed in Yellowstone. Although the park's land was protected, the animals living there were not. Grinnell wrote about the problem in a national article. The piece got the attention of the U.S. House of Representatives, and the following year, Congress passed the Yellowstone Park Protection Act of 1894. This act outlawed all hunting within the park's borders. Grinnell's work inspired many similar animal protection laws in other U.S. parks, including Glacier.

George Bird Grinnell

Grinnell also worried about how Native Americans were being treated in the West. He visited with tribes often, hunting and exploring with them. He saw their culture vanishing before his eyes and how poorly the Indian reservations were being managed by the U.S. government. He shared his concerns with others. In 1895, President Grover Cleveland put Grinnell in charge of working with the Blackfeet and Belknap tribes.

Thanks to his hard work, Grinnell became a well-known writer and editor. He became the editor of *Forest and Stream* magazine, and then started Forest and Stream Publishing. This company published books about the outdoors—many of these books are still read today.

Grinnell worked to protect Native American lands.

Grinnell's biggest goal was to teach the American people about the importance of conservation, or protecting nature. Later in life, Grinnell was honored at the White House for his work. President Calvin Coolidge told him, "Few have done so much as you, and none has done more."[1] The President praised Grinnell's efforts and added, "The Glacier National Park is peculiarly your monument."[2]

People had been drawn to northwest Montana for many years, even before Grinnell told them about its immense beauty. Native Americans lived on the land long before European settlers ever set foot on it. The Blackfeet lived on the prairies east of the mountains and to the west, the Salish and Kootenai occupied the valleys.

In later years, white hunters searching for beaver pelts roamed the wilderness. Next, miners arrived. They came in search of copper and gold. No large deposits were found, but several abandoned

The popular Forest and Stream magazine was published until 1930.

President Calvin Coolidge.

mineshafts can still be found within the park. The miners were followed by homesteaders, who created the first towns. When the Great Northern Railway opened in 1889, the area was open to anyone interested and willing to make the journey.

Long before anyone roamed these valleys, there were glaciers. More than 10,000 years ago, the earth was nearing the end of its last ice age. Ice in this part of the world measured one mile thick in certain places. As the ice melted and refroze over and

Kootenai people with their teepees and visitors in 1900.

The Great Northern Railway stretched across the northern United States. It started in St. Paul, Minnesota, wound west through North Dakota, Montana, and Northern Idaho, and ended in Everett and Seattle in Washington State.

over, it carved deep valleys. It left the rocky peaks that make up the park's landscape.

A little water hardly seems capable of creating the enormous stone structures like the ones in Glacier National Park. In large amounts, however, water can be one of the planet's most powerful forces. When it turns from liquid to ice and back again, the results can be catastrophic.

Water in the form of glaciers has carved several types of terrain into the mountainsides of Glacier National Park. Arêtes were formed where two glaciers once met. The ice on both sides of these mountain peaks

Ice caves are formed when water carves away the glacier from beneath.

wore away more and more land. Finally, only a knife-like ridge remained. This is how the famous Garden Wall was formed.

Like arêtes, horns are extremely steep peaks. They were formed by large glaciers scraping the mountainsides until they were completely vertical. Smaller glaciers also helped carve the steep sides through corries. Glaciers attached themselves to the mountainsides, creating heavy sections of ice.

Arêtes are knife-edge mountains.

Unlike regular ice, corries remained intact even when other ice melted away. Eventually, the weight of the corries forced them down the mountainsides, scraping away even more surface area.

Corries have dug out bowl-like areas in the terrain called cirques. These are often filled with the meltwaters from higher glaciers. These small

The Matterhorn is a large horn on the border of Italy and Switzerland.

The Lower Curtis Glacier in North Cascades National Park is a corrie. If the glacier melts, a lake may form in the cirque it has created.

Tarns are small lakes formed from melted glacial water.

lakes are called tarns. It is fairly common for tarns to feed into several lower bowls of water.

Hanging valleys were formed when one valley was cut across by another, deeper valley. This was how Bird Woman Falls was created. Hundreds of other waterfalls throughout the park are also the result of this type of erosion.

Bird Woman Falls graces a hanging valley.

BLACKFEET HISTORY

The Blackfeet people once controlled the area now known as Glacier National Park. Evidence shows they may have lived there for more than 10,000 years.[3] According to the tribe's ancient stories, the Blackfeet simply "woke up" there.

As hunters and gatherers, the Blackfeet most likely followed the buffalo herds. They used every part of the animals they caught: meat was used for food, hides were sewn into clothing or made into shelter with the animal's sinew, and bones were turned into weapons and tools. The Blackfeet set up their tents, or skin lodges, in minutes. They lived in them while they hunted, then, when food ran out, the Native Americans would take down their tents and move on to the next place.

A Blackfoot Warrior on Horseback *painted from life by Karl Bodmer, 1839.*

Chapter Three
GLACIER
WILDLIFE

One of the best things about visiting any one of the country's national parks is the abundance of plants and animals found there. This is certainly true in Glacier National Park. The area is home to seventy-one different types of mammals, as well as more than 260 species of birds. The smallest mammal is the pygmy shrew—it weighs the same as a dime! The largest is the grizzly bear. About 300 of them wander the park searching for some sweet huckleberries or green grass. Along with these mammals, the park is home to rabbits, bats, and rodents. This is the perfect place for several large cats, including bobcats, lynx, and mountain lions. The howl of a coyote can be heard, as well as the bark of a red fox. The park's mountains are home to mountain goats and bighorn sheep. The forests are full of deer, elk, moose, porcupines, chipmunks, and six types of squirrels.

Glacier National Park is home to many types of toads and frogs. The tailed frog lives near cold, bubbly

Mountain goats have adaptations that let them easily scale steep cliffs.

mountain streams. Two types of snakes can be found in the park, both garter snakes. The Western painted turtle also lives there. Its lower shell is bright orange and yellow, as if splashed by paint. The waters of the national park include trout, lake whitefish, and peamouth species.

Western painted turtle.

Insects are an important part of the park's balance. Army cutworm moths fly to the higher, cooler parts of the park. They are the perfect snack for hungry grizzly bears in late summer. Yellowstone checkerspot butterflies are found in several different areas of the park—their bright yellow spots can be seen

Butterflies like the checkerspot pollinate wildflowers in the park.

flickering through the forest as they search for bearberry plants. This is where they will lay their eggs.

Glacier National Park is also rich with birds. Clown ducks swim, dive, and explore creeks in search of food. The strange bird bobbing its head in and out of the water is a dipper. Dippers can swim underwater and even under the ice. On the tundra, the ptarmigan uses its feathered feet like a pair of snowshoes. It walks across the snow like an expert.

In addition to all the animals, nearly 2,000 species of plants help make up the park's vast ecosystem. From fragrant calypso orchids to tart huckleberries, the flora is delightful. The best-known plant is beargrass. It is neither bear food, nor grass. Instead, it is a member of the lily family. It is found at higher elevations. It was named by Meriwether Lewis during the famous Lewis and Clark expedition. Lewis thought the plant looked like a type of beargrass from his native Virginia.[1]

More than a thousand types of wildflowers

A ptarmigan.

Beargrass.

blanket the park in the spring and summer. Wildflowers even manage to grow up in the tundra where it is cold and windy. They grow close to the ground. Many have fine hairs that can trap what little heat there is. Others eat insects in order to stay healthy. A few types of flowers stay in seed form until a wildfire roars across the land. When the fires die down, the flowers burst out of the ground and fill the burned area with color and hope.

Wildflowers, like glacier lilies, paint the hills yellow when another spring arrives on the Logan Pass in the shadow of Mount Reynolds.

IS IT A GIANT CHIPMUNK? NO, IT'S A . . . SQUIRREL!

One of Glacier National Park's smallest residents is the golden-mantled ground squirrel. It looks like a huge chipmunk, but is actually a squirrel.

The park is also home to the northern flying squirrel. This squirrel cannot really fly, but it sure looks that way. The loose skin between the animal's legs allows it to glide through the air after jumping from a tree or other high perch. When fully outstretched, the skin looks like a cape. These squirrels are sometimes mistaken for bats, which also live in Glacier National Park.

A golden-mantled ground squirrel.

Flying squirrels glide through the air as they jump from tree to tree.

Chapter Four
FUN ALL YEAR ROUND

There is something for everyone all year round at Glacier National Park. Since the park is so large, the weather changes greatly from one area to the next. Altitude can create quite a difference in temperature. The eastern mountains are generally sunny but windy on summer days. The temperature may reach 90°F at this time. Once the sun sets, the temperature can drop to as low as 20°F.

During Glacier's winter months—late October through April—it is hard to believe visitors come here. The park is covered with several feet of frosty white snow. The setting takes on a whole new look and feeling when the white powder comes down from the mountains to dress the trees and meadows.

Some people enjoy deep snow and cold temperatures. Many are expert cross-country skiers or snowshoers. There are ski trails for every skill level—beginner to skilled. Winter hikers also enjoy pushing across the trails and leaving a line of footprints behind them. More experienced hikers might enjoy the glacier views from the

Even cold winter weather doesn't keep visitors away from the park.

Grinnell Complex trails, while newer hikers might prefer easier trails, such as those to Lake Josephine and Numa Ridge Lookout.

Some people visit the park in spring. It is often the most difficult time to stay because the weather is hard to predict. Unexpected snowstorms are common. When the snow begins to melt in the spring, the risk of an avalanche rises.

Summer is without a doubt the most popular time for tourists to travel to Glacier National Park. The sun is bright, the temperatures are warm, the scenery is spectacular and the roads are open. For those who prefer more scenery and fewer people, a backpacking trip is ideal.

There are more than 700 miles of hiking trails in Glacier Park.

The North Circle Route is considered one of the best hikes in the world. While it is only of medium difficulty, experts recommend taking seven days to complete its 52-mile length.

Backpacking trips should be matched to experience level. Skilled hikers may venture farther from the trail. Those who are new to hiking and camping will want to stay within a day's hike of a main route. Visitors can choose from over thirteen developed campgrounds with more than 1,000 campsites.

Going-to-the-Sun Road can be toured by bike or by vehicle.. The views are spectacular here!

Bicycle riders can travel along Going-to-the-Sun Road and enjoy a couple of perks that drivers don't. For example, bicyclists are allowed to travel the road before it is open to vehicles each spring.

Several stables within the park offer guided tours of the surrounding area on horseback. Like bicycles, horses can often go places that cars cannot. Stables also usually open around mid-May.

The Red Bus Tour takes visitors around in antique automobiles. Also called red jammers, they are the oldest fleet of passenger-carrying vehicles still in operation.[1] They earned the nickname because the cars' gears were known to jam as the climb on Going-to-the-Sun Road got steeper and steeper. The fleet of cars was completely rebuilt in 2001 and now run on propane. They can handle even the most challenging climb.

The wooden boats offering tours of Glacier National Park's many lakes are also rich in history. Some have been around since before the Great Depression of the 1930s. The scenery from the water is magnificent. Visitors

The famous Red Bus Tour takes visitors on the Going-to-the-Sun Road.

can also rent canoes, kayaks, rowboats, and motorboats to explore the lakes on their own.

Finally, tourists can take multi-day whitewater rafting trips down the waterways that run throughout the park. Rafting trips occur rain or shine during the summer months. Shorter, peaceful floats allowing visitors to enjoy the scenery are also available. For a little extra excitement, some tourists travel down the river in inflatable kayaks.

Whitewater rafts can take large groups of people.

PLEASE TAKE OUT THE TRASH

Remember that the animals are watching and waiting to see what you don't pick up!

Visitors to Glacier National Park are expected to carry out whatever they bring in. This helps keep the park free of litter. It also helps keep human visitors safe. Wild animals are attracted to the smell of garbage, particularly food waste. All leftover food items should be kept in sealed containers and taken home.

Chapter Five
A VIEW OF
THE
FUTURE

Ever since the late 1800s, the U.S. government has been establishing national parks. These parks protect wilderness areas for future generations.

At first, there was no plan in place for how to protect such huge areas of land. Big businesses, such as hotels, railroads, and sawmills, used the parks' resources for their own gain. Millionaire Stephen Mather wanted to change this. In 1915, he began speaking about how the country needed a National Park Service. It would protect the parks from companies that wanted to profit from the land and its resources.

Mather got support from other large businesses and newspapers, including the National Geographic Society. He talked to many students who wanted to be part of this program. By 1916, the National Park Service was officially established. Mather was its first director.

In 1995, David Barna became the Chief of Public Affairs for the National Park Service. He knew how much Americans loved the country's national parks. He said,

Grinnell Lake was named after George Bird Grinnell.

Stephen Mather.

"Americans developed a national pride of the natural wonders in this nation and they believed that they rivaled the great castles and cathedrals of Europe." Indeed, Americans care deeply about the parks. Recent years have brought a renewed sense of concern for the earth and its resources.

Rising temperatures are one of the biggest threats to Glacier National Park. The snow and ice are melting, and higher temperatures also bring less snow. Over the last century, the glaciers have been melting at an alarming rate. The park lost two glaciers just between 2005 and 2015. Scientists predict the glaciers will disappear completely by 2030. Some experts think they will be gone even sooner.[1]

Many scientists blame the huge thawing on global warming. High levels of carbon dioxide and other pollutants cause the earth's temperature to rise. Daniel Fagre is a U.S. Geological Survey (USGS) ecologist who works at the park. He reports that the threats of global warming are worse in certain areas than in others. "Mountain ecosystems have been changing about twice as fast as the rest of the globe. We have had temperature increases that are two times greater than the average."[2]

From 2008 until his retirement in 2012, Chas Cartwright was Glacier National Park's 21st superintendent. He believed the park's melting glaciers have helped Americans understand global warming. "Glacier

National Park has been the poster-child park for climate change for a lot of people in the country, and I think that there has been pretty sensational news about the glaciers disappearing in fairly short order."[3]

The disappearance of the glaciers is sure to have a big effect on the park's animals. For example, many plant and animal species living in the park's lakes are used to the cold water caused by the seasonal melting of the glaciers. Certain types of fish may be able to adapt to warmer temperatures, but if the smaller fish that it eats cannot survive the temperature change, the larger fish will starve. Over time, the

In 1850, there were about 150 glaciers in Glacier Park. By 1968, there were only fifty. By 2023, only twenty-five glaciers were left in the park.

disappearing glaciers could wipe out entire species that need the cold water in one way or another.

It is unlikely that any of the park's remaining glaciers can be saved—and this is alarming. It may be possible to slow down the melting. However, scientists say that even this is a long shot. Is it possible to make positive changes that will save the area from even more extreme climate change? Many scientists think so. First, people have to make these changes a priority.

Stephen Saunders is head of the Rocky Mountain Climate Organization. He wrote a report on how Glacier National Park is coping

Animals like the wolverine depend on snow to hide their dens. With decreasing snow cover, there will be fewer places to hide.

Scientists come to places like Melt Pond in Glacier National Park to study the effects of higher global temperatures. They search for ways to reverse the warming trend.

with the effects of climate change. He thinks it is important to see the opportunity, not just the loss. "We hope to raise awareness . . . ," he said, "that climate change is not just something happening to the polar ice caps. . . . It is affecting . . . places that are really special to the American people"—like Glacier National Park. Saunders hopes his report will help convince the public to do more to prevent global warming, and to protect Glacier.[4]

When it comes to the creatures living in Glacier National Park, there is good news and bad news. The good news is that most animal species are thriving in Glacier National Park today. The park was established

A brown bear heads for water from a waterfall in the park.

more than 100 years ago. This has given many animals the chance to reproduce successfully for years within the park's one million acres.

The bad news is that a few species are facing population challenges. The woodland caribou is at high risk of extinction in Canada. It is endangered and in serious decline in the United States. The gray wolf is also listed as endangered. The grizzly bear and the lynx are threatened. Unlike the receding glaciers, people *can* do something about these problems. Organizations, such as Defenders of Wildlife, work to save threatened and endangered species.

A WORLD BIOSPHERE RESERVE

Glacier National Park was named a world biosphere reserve in 1976. Like national parks, world biosphere reserves work to protect natural areas. They also do scientific research. Their work helps maintain the native plants and animals of these regions.

In recent years, the reserves have studied gray wolves, grizzly bears, and mountain goats. Experts want to find out how tourism and pollution might be affecting these animals and the places they live.

Even groundhogs enjoy Glacier's mountain views.

FUN FACTS

- Glacier National Park was established on May 11, 1910.

- President Woodrow Wilson signed the act that established the National Park Service on August 25, 1916.

- Waterton-Glacier International Peace Park was established in 1932. The construction on the Going-to-the-Sun Road was completed the following year in 1933.

- Going-to-the-Sun Road runs east to west through the park. It is about fifty miles long.

- Glacier National Park became a World Biosphere Reserve in 1976.

- The park covers 1,012,837 acres, or 1,583 square miles.

- Glacier has 175 mountains. The tallest of these is Mount Cleveland, at 10,466 feet in elevation.

- Glacier National Park has 762 lakes, but only 131 of them have been named.

- Its largest lake is Lake McDonald. This body of water measures 9.94 miles long, one mile wide, and 464 feet deep.

- Glacier National Park is home to sixty-eight types of mammals.

- It contains more than 260 different bird species.

- Nearly 2,000 plant species can be found in the park.

- In 1850, the park had a total of 150 glaciers. By 2015, it had only twenty-five glaciers.

- The largest glacier in the park is Blackfoot Glacier. It measures 0.7 square miles.

Chapter 1. The Crown of the Continent

1. National Park Service. "Glacier National Park Fact Sheet." http://www.nps. gov/glac/parknews/fact-sheet.htm.

2. Oswald, Michael Joseph. *Your Guide to the National Parks.* Whitelaw, WI: Stone Road Press, 2012, p. 259.

Chapter 2. Creating a National Park

1. McCabe, Richard E. "George Bird Grinnell, 'The Noblest Roman of Them All,' " Outdoor Writers Association of America—http://owaa.org/owaa-legends/ george-bird-grinnell-the-noblest-roman-of-them-all/.

2. Ibid.

3. National Park Service. "Glacier National Park: Introduction to Native American Units." http://www.nps.gov/glac/forteachers/intro-to-native-american.htm.

Chapter 3. Glacier Wildlife

1. Hiking in Glacier. http://www.hikinginglacier.com

Chapter 5. A View of the Future

1. Ellis, Jessica. "Montana's Melting Glaciers: The Poster-Child for Climate Change." *CNN*, October 6, 2010.

2. Ibid.

3. Ibid.

4. Repanshek, Kurt. "Climate Change Continues to Melt Glacier National Park's Icons." *National Parks Traveler*, April 12, 2010. http://www.nationalparkstraveler.com/2010/04/ climate-change-continues-melt-glacier-national-parks-icons5669

Works Consulted

Allen, Thomas B., et al. *Guide to National Parks of the United States.* Washington, DC: National Geographic, 2012.

McCabe, Richard E. "George Bird Grinnell, 'The Noblest Roman of Them All.'" Outdoor Writers Association of America.

Molvar, Eric. *Hiking Glacier and Waterton Lakes National Parks.* Helena, MT: Globe Pequot Press, 2012.

Montana: Official State Travel Site. http://www.visitmt.com/

National Park Service. http://www.nps.gov/index.htm

National Parks Traveler. http://www.nationalparkstraveler.com/

Oswald, Michael Joseph. *Your Guide to the National Parks.* Whitelaw, WI: Stone Road Press, 2012.

A Slow Hiker's Guide™ to Glacier National Park.

Books

Aretha, David. *Glacier National Park.* Berkeley Heights, NJ: Enslow Publishers, 2009.

Flynn, Sarah Wassner. *National Parks Guide USA.* Washington, DC: National Geographic Kids, 2012.

Lasky, Kathryn. *John Muir: America's First Environmentalist.* Somerville, MA: Candlewick Press, 2014.

Love, Donna. *The Totally Out There Guide to Glacier National Park.* Missoula, MT: Mountain Press Publishing Company, 2010.

McCarthy, Pat. *Friends of the Earth: A History of American Environmentalism with 21 Activities.* Chicago: Chicago Review Press, 2013.

Otfinoski, Steven. *Grover Cleveland (Presidents and Their Times)*. Tarrytown, NY: Benchmark Books, 2010.

Websites
Defenders of Wildlife
    http://www.defenders.org/
National Park Service, Glacier National Park, Park Fun
    http://www.nps.gov/glac/forkids/parkfun.htm

arête (ah-RET)—A sharp ridge separating two glacial valleys in mountainous regions.

avalanche (AV-uh-lantch)—The sudden falling or sliding of a large mass of snow and ice.

cirque (SIRK)—A steep-walled semicircular valley, carved by a glacier, that may contain a lake.

conservation (kon-ser-VAY-shun)—The official care and protection of rivers, forests, and other natural resources.

corrie (KOR-ee)—A small glacier-type mass of ice that creates steep slopes around cirques.

crevasse (kruh-VAHS)—A deep gap in glacial ice.

disposable (dih-SPOH-zuh-bul)—Designed to be thrown away after use.

ecosystem (EK-oh-sis-tum)—All the plants and animals that live together within a specific environment.

erosion (ee-ROH-zhun)—The wearing away of land by wind, water, or ice.

global warming (GLOH-bul WAR-ming)—The gradual rise in the temperature of Earth's atmosphere caused largely by excess carbon dioxide and other pollution.

homesteading (HOHM-sted-ing)—A federal program that helped settlers develop farmland during the middle 1800s.

horn—In geology, a steep mountain peak formed by glaciers.

naturalist (NATCH-ruh-list)—A person who studies living things and their environment.

ornithology (or-nih-THOL-uh-jee)—The study of birds.

reservation (rez-er-VAY-shun)—An area set aside for use by a Native American tribe or nation.

superintendent (SOO-per-in-TEN-dent)—The person who oversees managers and other employees.

tarn—A small mountain lake or pool that has very steep banks.

topography (tah-POG-ruh-fee)—Detailed mapping of the ground.

PHOTO CREDITS: P.1—Tobias Klenze; pp. 9, 22, 23, 28, 30, 33, 37, 39, 40, 45—NPS.gov; p. 9—Esther Lee; pp. 15, 16—loc.gov, NPS.gov; pp. 16, 17—camptocamp; p. 17—Richard Allaway; p. 18—J. Brew, wp8thsub; p. 20—Katy Brady; p. 22—Bill Bouton; p. 24—Dave Restivo; p. 25—Shanthanu Bhardwaj; p. 26—David Restivo; pp. 31—locosteve; p. 35—Ryan McKee; p. 38—Uusijani; 43—Anselm Hook. All other photos—Public Domain. Every measure has been taken to find all copyright holders of material used in this book. In the event any mistakes or omissions have happened within, attempts to correct them will be made in future editions of the book.

Index